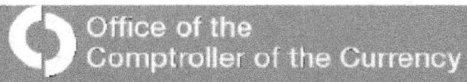

I0439720

2013 Survey of Credit Underwriting Practices

Office of the Comptroller of the Currency
Washington, D.C.

January 2014

Contents

Introduction

The Office of the Comptroller of the Currency (OCC) conducted its 19th annual "Survey of Credit Underwriting Practices" to identify trends in lending standards and credit risk for the most common types of commercial and retail credit offered by national banks and federal savings associations (collectively, banks). The survey covers the 18-month period ending June 30, 2013.

The 2013 survey presents OCC examiner assessments of credit underwriting standards at 86 banks with assets of $3 billion or more. Examiners reported on loan products for each company whose loan volume was 2 percent or more of its committed loan portfolio, or greater than $10 billion in committed exposure. The OCC recognizes that banks offer many other loan products not meeting these size thresholds; that information, however, was not collected for this report. The survey covers loans totaling $4.5 trillion representing 87 percent of total loans in the federal banking system. Large banks discussed in this report are the 19 largest banks by asset size supervised by the OCC's Large Bank Supervision Department; the other 67 banks are supervised by the OCC's Midsize and Community Bank Supervision Department.

OCC examiners assigned to each bank assessed overall credit trends for 18 commercial and retail credit products. For the purposes of this survey, commercial credit includes 11 categories:

- Agricultural
- Asset-based
- Commercial leasing
- Commercial real estate (CRE) construction
- International
- Large corporate
- Leveraged
- Middle market
- Other commercial real estate
- Residential construction
- Small business

Retail credit includes seven categories:

- Affordable housing
- Conventional home equity
- Credit cards
- Direct consumer
- High loan-to-value (HLTV) home equity
- Indirect consumer
- Residential first mortgages

Underwriting standards, as presented in this report, refer to the terms and conditions under which banks extend or renew credit, such as financial reporting and collateral requirements, repayment programs, terms, pricing, and covenants. Conclusions about easing or tightening represent OCC examiners' observations during the 18-month survey period ending June 30, 2013. A conclusion that underwriting standards for a particular loan category eased or tightened does not necessarily indicate an adjustment in all of the standards for that particular product. Rather, the conclusion indicates that the adjustments that did occur had the net effect of easing or tightening the aggregate conditions under which banks extended credit.

Part I of this report summarizes the overall findings of the survey. Part II shows the findings in data tables and graphs. Part III presents the raw data used to develop the survey's principal findings and to create the data tables and graphs. (Note: Some percentages in tables and graphs do not add to 100 because of rounding.)

Part I: Overall Results

Primary Findings

- The results of this year's survey show that underwriting standards continued to ease within both commercial and retail products. Examiners reported that banks that eased standards generally did so in response to changes in economic outlook, an increasingly competitive environment, plentiful market liquidity, and changes in the bank's risk appetite including a desire for growth. Large banks reported the highest share of eased underwriting standards across loan categories. Notwithstanding these trends, examiners reported that most banks maintained good or satisfactory adherence to underwriting standards.

- Loan portfolios that experienced the most easing in underwriting standards include indirect consumer, credit cards, large corporate, asset-based lending, international, and leveraged loans, continuing a trend noted last year. Reduced collateral requirements, loosening covenants, and scorecard cutoffs were the primary methods that banks used to ease standards. Loan portfolios that experienced the most tightening in underwriting since last year include HLTV home equity and conventional home equity.

- As in the past, the economy's health was a major factor influencing changes in underwriting standards. Expectations regarding the future health of the economy, however, differ by bank and loan product as examiners reported that the economic outlook was one of the main reasons given for both easing and tightening of underwriting standards. Other factors influencing tighter underwriting standards were changes in risk appetite for both commercial and retail products and changes in regulatory policies around retail products.

- No banks tightened small business banking underwriting practices, with 79 percent of banks reporting unchanged standards from the last survey and 21 percent of banks reporting eased standards. The level of credit risk in small business loans remained stable, although there is an expectation by examiners that the level of credit risk for this product will increase at 32 percent of banks over the next 12 months.

- Since the 2012 survey, changes in the level of credit risk were mixed in commercial and retail portfolios. Approximately 16 percent of all commercial and retail loan products show increased credit risk, 59 percent show the same level of credit risk, and 25 percent indicate decreased credit risk when compared with 18 months ago. Over the next 12 months, examiners believe that credit risk will likely increase for 30 percent of the loan products, decrease for 17 percent, and remain unchanged for 53 percent.

- Similar to the 2012 survey results, this year's survey indicates that the majority of banks generally apply the same underwriting standards to loans underwritten with the intent to hold as to those underwritten with the intent to sell, although some variance was noted in leveraged loans and international loans. Examiners largely cited good or satisfactory adherence to underwriting standards. Underwriting policy exceptions, although increasing, were well supported.

Commentary on Credit Risk and Underwriting

Credit risk has stabilized but remains significant. Easing underwriting standards combined with expected loan growth is also contributing to slowly increasing credit risk concerns. Although traditional credit-risk indicators are stabilizing, loosening underwriting standards in a competitive market generally adds risk back into the system.

The most important credit-related issue identified by examiners for banks of all sizes is the easing of underwriting standards in response to competitive pressures and a desire to achieve loan growth and increase earnings. Against this backdrop, banks eased their underwriting standards from the prior year in response to significant competition for limited borrower loan demand making it difficult to achieve loan growth goals. A smaller number of banks tightened standards since the prior year. Other important credit-related issues noted in the survey by examiners include maintaining satisfactory risk selection criteria and sound credit risk management practices against ongoing economic and competitive pressures.

Overall, examiners reported a continued net easing of underwriting standards. While the majority of standards remain unchanged (64 percent for commercial and 68 percent for retail), easing of overall commercial underwriting standards (reported in 28 percent of the banks) doubled since last year. Easing of overall retail underwriting standards increased to 22 percent of the banks from 15 percent in the prior year. Loan products that experienced the most easing were asset-based lending, credit cards, indirect consumer, international, large corporate, and leveraged loans. Changes in collateral requirements and covenants were the primary methods that banks used to ease underwriting standards for commercial products. Changes in collateral requirements and scorecard cutoffs resulted in eased underwriting standards for retail products. In addition, examiners reported a trend of increasing policy exceptions in commercial and retail products.

There was a lower level of tightening underwriting standards compared with 2012, with commercial products tightened in 8 percent of the banks, and retail underwriting standards tightened in 10 percent of the banks. Loan products with the most tightening were primarily the retail-related products of HLTV home equity and conventional home equity. For banks that tightened commercial standards, reasons noted were changing risk appetite along with increased use of covenants and collateral. Changing risk appetite and regulatory requirements were reasons for tightening of retail loan standards, with increased documentation and debt service requirements noted as the most common methods to tighten these standards.

The survey indicates that 70 percent of examiner responses expect that the overall level of credit risk will either remain unchanged or increase over the next 12 months. This represents a decline from last year's survey, which indicated that 77 percent of examiner responses showed an expectation for no change or an increase in the level of credit risk over the next 12 months. In instances when examiners expect risk to increase, their primary reasons for the increase were changes in the state of the economy and continued strong competition.

As banks continue to ease underwriting standards, they should maintain prudent standards. The OCC expects banks to underwrite loans based on sound underwriting standards, regardless of the intent to hold or sell the loan, and to apply the same general standards for both types of lending.

Commercial Underwriting Standards

The number of banks where examiners report a net easing in commercial credit standards doubled from 2012. As presented in table 1, the survey results indicate that the majority of banks (64 percent) show unchanged underwriting standards while 28 percent of banks eased underwriting standards. The easing of standards occurred mainly in large banks.

Table 1: Overall Commercial Product Underwriting Trends

	2006	2007	2008	2009	2010	2011	2012	2013
Eased	31%	26%	6%	0%	2%	20%	14%	28%
Unchanged	63%	58%	42%	14%	33%	48%	70%	64%
Tightened	6%	16%	52%	86%	65%	32%	16%	8%

For additional information, see figure 1 on page 13.

Underwriting standards are easing due to increased competition, a desire for loan growth, ample market liquidity, and the economic outlook. Examiners reported that for the 8 percent of products where standards tightened, the predominant reasons for tightening relate to the economic outlook and changes in risk appetite for the bank. Examiners also reported that banks continue to have mixed expectations for the future; some banks cited an improving economic outlook as a reason for easing underwriting standards, while others cited an uncertain economic outlook as a reason for tightening standards. The available liquidity in secondary markets contributed to easing standards in leveraged finance, asset-based loans, international, and large corporate loans.

In this year's survey, increased competition in commercial loan products lowered pricing, increased credit availability, relaxed loan covenants, and lengthened maturities. This continued a trend noted in last year's survey. The OCC expects banks to maintain prudent underwriting standards, especially in line with heightened competition and strong market liquidity.

Notwithstanding these trends, examiners largely cited good or satisfactory adherence to underwriting standards and observed well-supported underwriting exceptions when exceptions were noted. For 84 percent of commercial products, the level of approved exceptions decreased or had no change. Underwriting exception tracking is in place for 95 percent of the loan products.

The direction of credit risk across the 86 banks moved from largely unchanged or decreasing to primarily unchanged since the prior year. Fifty-three percent of examiner responses indicate the risk levels for 2014 are expected to remain unchanged, while 31 percent expect risk to increase. Examiner expectations are consistent with broad commercial credit quality trends, which generally show stabilization or a slow improvement. Leveraged and international loans reflected moderately increasing levels of credit risk, while leasing, CRE, and large corporate loans reflected net decreasing levels of risk.

Selected Product Trends

Underwriting eased for most commercial products, with more significant easing identified in leveraged, international, large corporate, and asset-based lending. Large banks typically offered the products with the most easing.

CRE

CRE products include commercial construction, residential construction, and all other CRE loans. Almost all surveyed banks offered at least one type of CRE product. While the majority of banks' underwriting standards remained unchanged for CRE, a declining percentage of banks continued to tighten standards across all three CRE products, while an increasing percentage of banks eased standards in commercial construction and other CRE. Examiners cite the competition in the real estate market, product performance, risk appetite, change in market strategy, and increased liquidity as the main reasons for banks' net easing of standards. Examiners indicate current underwriting standards for CRE products remained either conservative at 54 percent or moderate at 36 percent.

The level and direction of credit risk in CRE categories showed increasing credit risk for commercial construction and other CRE, as banks increase their level of lending in these products. Increased credit risks were attributed to continued economic weakness, strong competition, a change in strategy, and changes in risk appetite. Examiner expectations for risk in the next 12 months show an increasing level of risk in 26 percent of commercial construction, 38 percent of residential construction, and 35 percent of other CRE. Tables 2, 3, and 4 provide breakdowns by real estate type, and tables 22, 24, and 26 provide additional detail on risk.

Thirty-five banks (41 percent) offered commercial construction loans. For those banks that offered commercial construction loans, table 2 shows that underwriting standards for commercial construction remain unchanged at 71 percent of banks, tightened at 11 percent, and eased at 18 percent.

Table 2: CRE Lending: Commercial Construction

	2006	2007	2008	2009	2010	2011	2012	2013
Eased	32%	28%	8%	0%	3%	3%	5%	18%
Unchanged	56%	59%	43%	20%	25%	61%	75%	71%
Tightened	12%	13%	49%	80%	72%	36%	20%	11%

For additional information, see tables on page 28.

Fourteen banks (16 percent) offered residential construction loan products. Performance of these products remained weak, and many banks have either exited the product or significantly curtailed new originations. Table 3 shows that underwriting standards were unchanged for 92 percent of banks offering the residential construction product in 2013 and tightened at 8 percent of the banks. No banks reported easing standards.

Table 3: CRE Lending: Residential Construction

	2006	2007	2008	2009	2010	2011	2012	2013
Eased	25%	17%	2%	0%	0%	0%	0%	0%
Unchanged	64%	50%	36%	8%	36%	63%	79%	92%
Tightened	11%	33%	62%	92%	64%	37%	21%	8%

For additional information, see tables on page 29.

Seventy-five banks (87 percent) offered a variety of CRE loans for purposes other than residential or commercial construction. For purposes of this survey, the OCC broadly grouped these loans under an "other" category. As described earlier, 35 percent of examiner responses expect that risk will increase over the next 12 months based on concerns with the economic environment, collateral values, and easing underwriting standards. Table 4 shows that 24 percent of banks offering other CRE loans eased underwriting standards, while 8 percent tightened standards, and 68 percent left underwriting standards unchanged.

Table 4: CRE Lending: Other

	2006	2007	2008	2009	2010	2011	2012	2013
Eased	32%	20%	2%	2%	2%	9%	12%	24%
Unchanged	60%	73%	73%	22%	38%	58%	76%	68%
Tightened	8%	7%	25%	76%	60%	33%	12%	8%

For additional information, see tables on page 30.

Leveraged Lending

While only 16 large or midsize banks (19 percent) offered leveraged loans, the size of the portfolio is significant relative to total outstanding loans because of the dollar size of transactions. Table 5 shows that 53 percent of banks offering leveraged loans eased underwriting standards; none reported tightening standards; and 47 percent of the banks left underwriting standards unchanged. Easing of standards is attributed to increased competition, changing economic conditions, and ample market liquidity. This is the third consecutive year for which examiners reported significant continued easing.

Examiners also reported that the level of credit risk in leveraged loans increased in 40 percent of banks offering leveraged loans and remained unchanged in 47 percent. Thirteen percent reported that the level of credit risk decreased somewhat. Examiners expect that in 93 percent of the banks offering leveraged loans, the level of credit risk in this product will likely remain unchanged or increase over the next year. Increases are anticipated from strong competition and increasing market liquidity driven by banks' and investors' pursuit of growth in earning assets. Examiners will monitor this expected trend closely, as such pressures could result in further easing of underwriting standards, lower pricing, and fewer or no covenants.

Table 5: Leveraged Lending

	2006	2007	2008	2009	2010	2011	2012	2013
Eased	61%	67%	20%	0%	0%	37%	38%	53%
Unchanged	31%	33%	20%	31%	25%	44%	62%	47%
Tightened	8%	0%	60%	69%	75%	19%	0%	0%

For additional information, see tables on page 33.

Small Business Loans

Forty-five of the surveyed banks (52 percent) offer small business loans, and the number of banks that have eased standards returned to 2006 levels. Table 6 shows 21 percent of banks eased underwriting standards, and 79 percent kept underwriting the same. No banks were noted to have tightened standards. Increased competition and market strategy were the primary reasons for changes in credit underwriting standards.

Examiners indicated that the level of small business credit risk declined or remained relatively unchanged at 81 percent of the banks and expect the level of risk will continue to decline or remain the same over the next year in 68 percent of the banks offering the product. Changes in economic conditions and market strategy were most frequently reported as reasons for the reduced level of risk. See table 36 for additional information on risk.

Table 6: Small Business Loans

	2006	2007	2008	2009	2010	2011	2012	2013
Eased	19%	11%	11%	0%	0%	12%	9%	21%
Unchanged	76%	76%	72%	36%	34%	55%	82%	79%
Tightened	5%	13%	17%	64%	66%	33%	9%	0%

For additional information, see tables on page 35.

Originate to Hold Versus Originate to Sell

The OCC expects banks to underwrite loans based on sound underwriting standards, regardless of the intent to hold or sell loans, and to apply the same general standards for both types of lending.

Of the loan products surveyed, 18 percent were originated to sell. The largest categories of loans in this group were leveraged loans, large corporate loans, international credits, asset-based loans, and commercial leasing. As shown in table 7, there has been continued improvement since 2008 in reducing the differences in hold versus sell underwriting standards. The OCC continues to monitor and assess any differences in underwriting standards for loans that banks intend to sell versus those they intend to hold.

Table 7: Hold Versus Sell Underwriting Standards

Product	Underwritten differently					
	2008	2009	2010	2011	2012	2013
Leveraged loans	67%	38%	12%	13%	15%	13%
International	40%	0%	10%	11%	9%	7%
CRE—commercial construction	20%	10%	0%	0%	0%	2%
Large corporate	21%	21%	3%	3%	3%	0%
CRE—other	20%	9%	0%	0%	1%	0%
Asset-based loans	33%	13%	0%	0%	0%	0%
CRE—residential construction	17%	17%	0%	0%	0%	0%

Retail Underwriting Standards

Of the 86 banks that participated in the survey, 84 underwrite one or more of the seven retail loan products, with residential real estate loans making up the largest share of the banks' portfolios, followed by home equity loans. Among surveyed banks, the size of their retail portfolios declined relative to the total portfolio of loans covered in the survey.

As shown in table 8, examiners reported a continued slow trend toward easing underwriting standards as the percent of banks easing standards rose to 22 percent from 15 percent at the last survey. At the same time, at the majority of banks (68 percent), standards remain unchanged while standards tightened at 10 percent of banks. Examiners attributed the easing to improving economic trends, changes in market strategy, risk appetite, and product performance. Good or acceptable adherence to underwriting standards was noted, with exceptions well supported for the majority of products. Exception tracking is in place for 95 percent of the individual retail products, representing an increase of almost 10 percent from 2012. Examiners report that 73 percent of the banks surveyed do not plan to introduce any new products during the next year.

Table 8: Overall Retail Product Underwriting Trends

	2006	2007	2008	2009	2010	2011	2012	2013
Eased	28%	20%	0%	0%	0%	7%	15%	22%
Unchanged	65%	67%	32%	17%	26%	63%	63%	68%
Tightened	7%	13%	68%	83%	74%	30%	22%	10%

For additional information, see figure 7 on page 20.

The direction of credit risk for individual retail products showed further improvement from the previous survey, with examiners reporting mild to no concern. Individual retail products that saw an increase in the level of credit risk were indirect consumer loans; the increase was primarily due to changes in underwriting standards, underwriting practices, and risk selection criteria. Although examiners reported the direction of risk increased in select individual retail products, the overall trend in credit risk levels improved from last year. Twenty-three percent of examiners expect the credit risk in retail portfolios will increase over the next 12 months, while 73 percent expect the level of credit risk for retail products will decrease or experience no change.

Examiners reported that the most important credit-related issues in retail products centered on increased competition causing pressure on underwriting standards and risk selection criteria, ongoing weaknesses in certain economic sectors, and maintaining sufficient controls with increased growth. Secondary issues varied, as examiners reported that community banks are challenged in effectively merging new acquisitions into existing platforms under existing risk management structures. Midsize and large banks are focused on designing long-term strategic plans, effecting problem asset resolution, assessing representation and warranty liability, evaluating rising interest rates, and dealing prudently with competitive pressures to ease credit standards.

Selected Product Trends

The following sections discuss changes within various product types.

Residential Real Estate

Seventy-eight of the surveyed banks (91 percent) originated residential real estate loans. As shown in table 9, there is a continued trend from tightening to unchanged standards, with 76 percent of the banks reporting unchanged residential real estate underwriting standards. Although the housing market experienced a noticeable recovery since the last survey, two banks exited the residential real estate business during the past year. Examiners reported, however, that no banks plan to exit the business in the coming year. Additionally, examiners indicated that the level of risk in these portfolios remained unchanged or decreased at 87 percent of the banks. See table 50 for additional detail.

Table 9: Residential Real Estate Lending

	2006	2007	2008	2009	2010	2011	2012	2013
Eased	26%	19%	0%	0%	5%	8%	10%	11%
Unchanged	69%	67%	44%	27%	36%	52%	65%	76%
Tightened	5%	14%	56%	73%	59%	40%	25%	13%

For additional information, see tables on page 42.

As shown in table 10, similar results were noted for conventional home equity loans, with 73 percent of banks keeping underwriting standards unchanged, and 5 percent easing standards. Examiner responses show that the level of risk for the next 12 months is expected to decline or remain unchanged at 87 percent of banks that offer this product. See table 40 for additional detail.

Table 10: Conventional Home Equity

	2006	2007	2008	2009	2010	2011	2012	2013
Eased	34%	19%	2%	0%	5%	9%	18%	5%
Unchanged	64%	65%	46%	22%	35%	55%	68%	73%
Tightened	2%	16%	52%	78%	60%	36%	14%	22%

For additional information, see tables on page 37.

Since the 2012 survey, of the four banks that originated HLTV home equity loans, two banks have exited the business and one plans to exit the business in the coming year. Table 11 shows that the remaining banks are equally reflecting unchanged or tightened underwriting standards, with no banks easing standards. Examiners expect the level of risk over the next 12 months to decline or remain unchanged at all banks. See table 46 for additional detail.

Table 11: High Loan-to-Value Home Equity

	2006	2007	2008	2009	2010	2011	2012	2013
Eased	37%	22%	6%	0%	0%	0%	17%	0%
Unchanged	63%	61%	6%	7%	13%	50%	17%	50%
Tightened	0%	17%	88%	93%	87%	50%	66%	50%

For additional information, see tables on page 40.

Credit Cards

Twenty-one of the surveyed banks (24 percent) offered credit cards. Table 12 shows that underwriting standards remained largely unchanged at 54 percent of the banks since the last survey, and the percentage of banks that eased underwriting standards decreased from 2012. Examiners attributed the easing of standards to changes in economic outlook, product performance, market strategy, and risk appetite. The primary methods used for easing credit underwriting standards were changes in the credit line, pricing and fees, scorecard cutoffs, debt-to-income ratios, and documentation requirements.

Credit risk in the card portfolios has stabilized; examiners reported no change in the level of credit risk at 46 percent of the banks and a decrease in the level of credit risk at 33 percent of the banks. In the next 12 months, examiners expect the level of credit risk to remain stable or decrease somewhat at 63 percent of the banks. Examiners reported increased exposure to credit card portfolios at four banks since the last survey and noted that four banks plan to significantly increase exposure in the next 12 months. Examiners reported being mildly concerned with the direction of credit risk at 50 percent of the banks. One company has left the business since last year, and none plan to exit this line of business in the coming year. Examiners noted that increased competition from new companies and "re-entrants" is forcing continued easing of standards in order to maintain market share.

Table 12: Credit Card Lending

	2006	2007	2008	2009	2010	2011	2012	2013
Eased	19%	16%	18%	0%	0%	25%	35%	33%
Unchanged	56%	79%	47%	32%	19%	31%	50%	54%
Tightened	25%	5%	35%	68%	81%	44%	15%	13%

For additional information, see tables on page 38.

Consumer Lending (Direct and Indirect)

Direct and indirect consumer lending encompasses a variety of products, with banks taking different actions with regard to underwriting standards or plans for each product in this section. Indirect lending is generally dominated by auto loans but can also include other products such as student, marine, and recreational vehicle loans. Examiners' conclusions about credit risk or the direction of credit risk may not be the same for all products grouped in this section. When differences exist, the response generally relates to the most significant product by dollar volume.

During the survey period, 25 banks (29 percent) and 24 banks (28 percent) participated in direct and indirect lending, respectively. Thirty-three percent of the banks participating in direct consumer lending and 58 percent of those originating indirect consumer lending plan to increase their exposure to these products in the coming year.

As shown in table 13, underwriting standards eased in 8 percent of the direct consumer lending banks, while 85 percent of those banks kept their standards unchanged. Seven percent of the banks tightened standards. Examiners reported that the level of credit risk in direct lending portfolios was unchanged at 85 percent of the banks, with 18 percent of examiner responses expecting credit risk to increase in the next 12 months. See table 44 for additional detail.

Table 13: Direct Consumer Lending

	2006	2007	2008	2009	2010	2011	2012	2013
Eased	3%	8%	6%	4%	0%	10%	12%	8%
Unchanged	91%	87%	72%	28%	68%	75%	88%	85%
Tightened	6%	5%	22%	68%	32%	15%	0%	7%

For additional information, see tables on page 39.

Table 14 shows 63 percent of banks eased underwriting standards for indirect lending. The easing was attributed to changes in the economic outlook, competitive environment, market strategy, risk appetite, and changes in product performance. The underwriting standards that changed for these products are primarily the maximum size of the credit line, pricing and fees, collateral requirements, advance rates, amortization requirements, maximum maturity, scorecard cutoffs, and debt-to-income. Twenty-nine percent of banks' standards for indirect lending remained unchanged, while 8 percent tightened standards.

Additional indirect lending information in table 48 reflects examiner views that 58 percent of banks had an increase in the level of credit risk in the indirect portfolio. The primary reasons for increased credit risk were changes in underwriting standards, external conditions, risk selection, and underwriting practices. Examiners indicate they expect that 66 percent of banks with indirect lending portfolios will have an increase in the level of credit risk over the next 12 months.

Table 14: Indirect Consumer Lending

	2006	2007	2008	2009	2010	2011	2012	2013
Eased	35%	16%	20%	0%	5%	37%	60%	63%
Unchanged	52%	75%	56%	26%	33%	47%	35%	29%
Tightened	13%	9%	24%	74%	62%	16%	5%	8%

For additional information, see tables on page 41.

Originate to Hold Versus Originate to Sell

Banks originated 77 percent of retail products to hold, while the balance was originated to sell. The most popular retail product to sell was residential real estate loans, while the most common product to hold was conventional home equity loans, followed closely by direct and indirect consumer loans, and credit cards. The OCC continues to monitor and assess any difference in underwriting standards for loans that banks intend to hold versus those they intend to sell.

Part II: Data Graphs

Some percentages used to create the data graphs do not add to 100 because of rounding.

Figure 1: Overall Commercial Credit Underwriting Trends (Percentage of Responses)

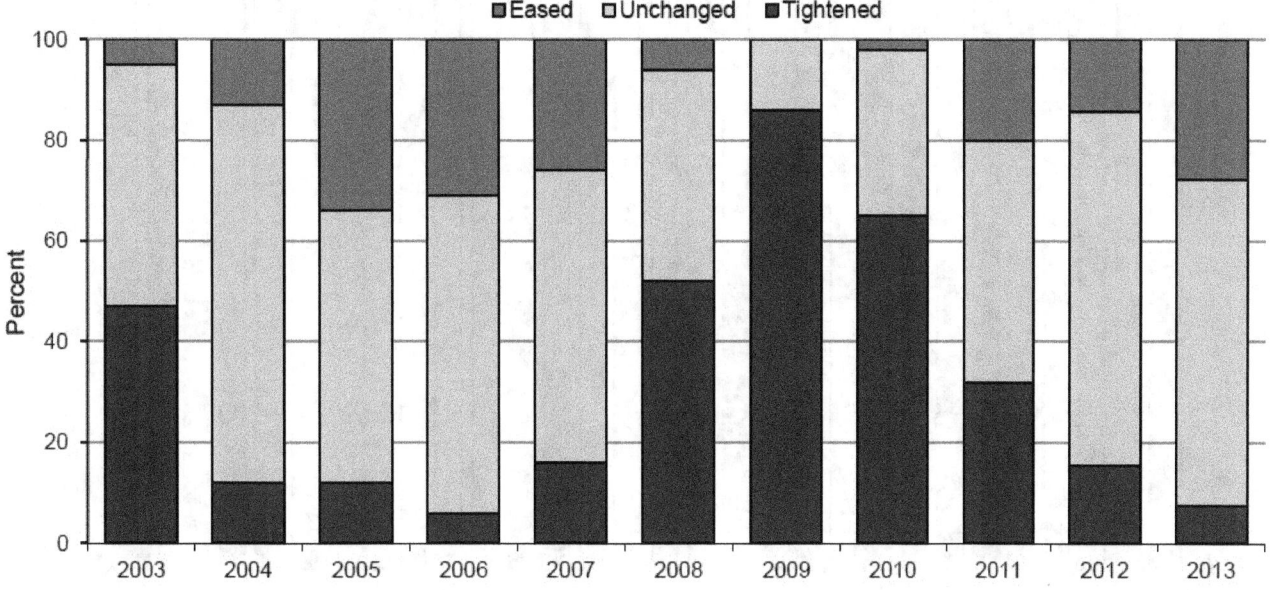

Figure 2: Commercial Underwriting Trends, by Product Type

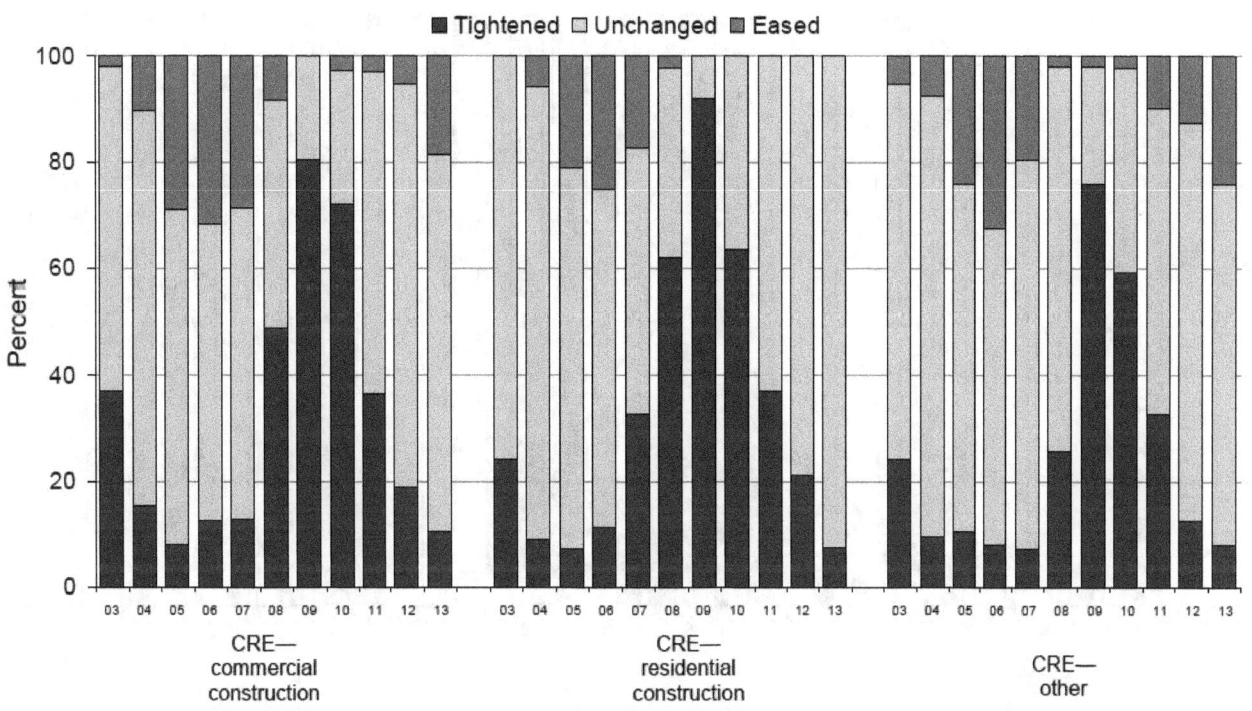

Figure 2 (cont.): Commercial Underwriting Trends, by Product Type

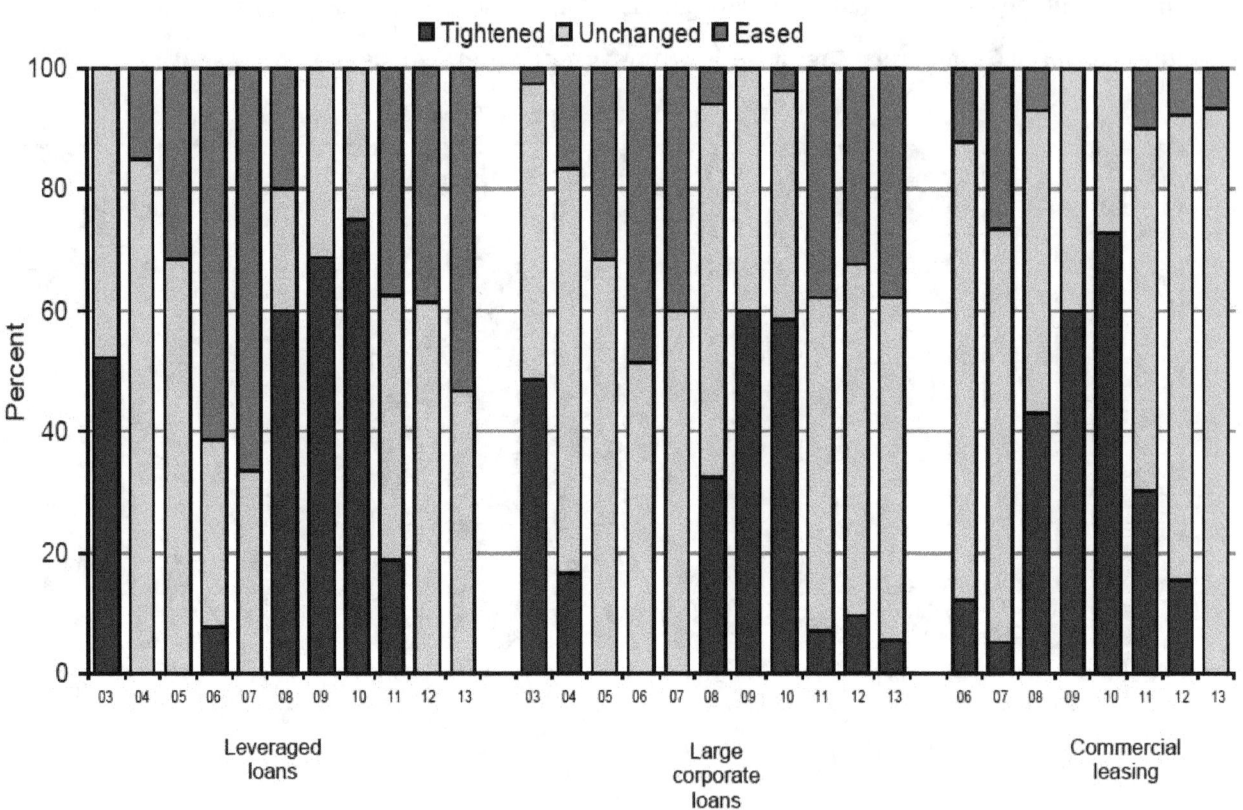

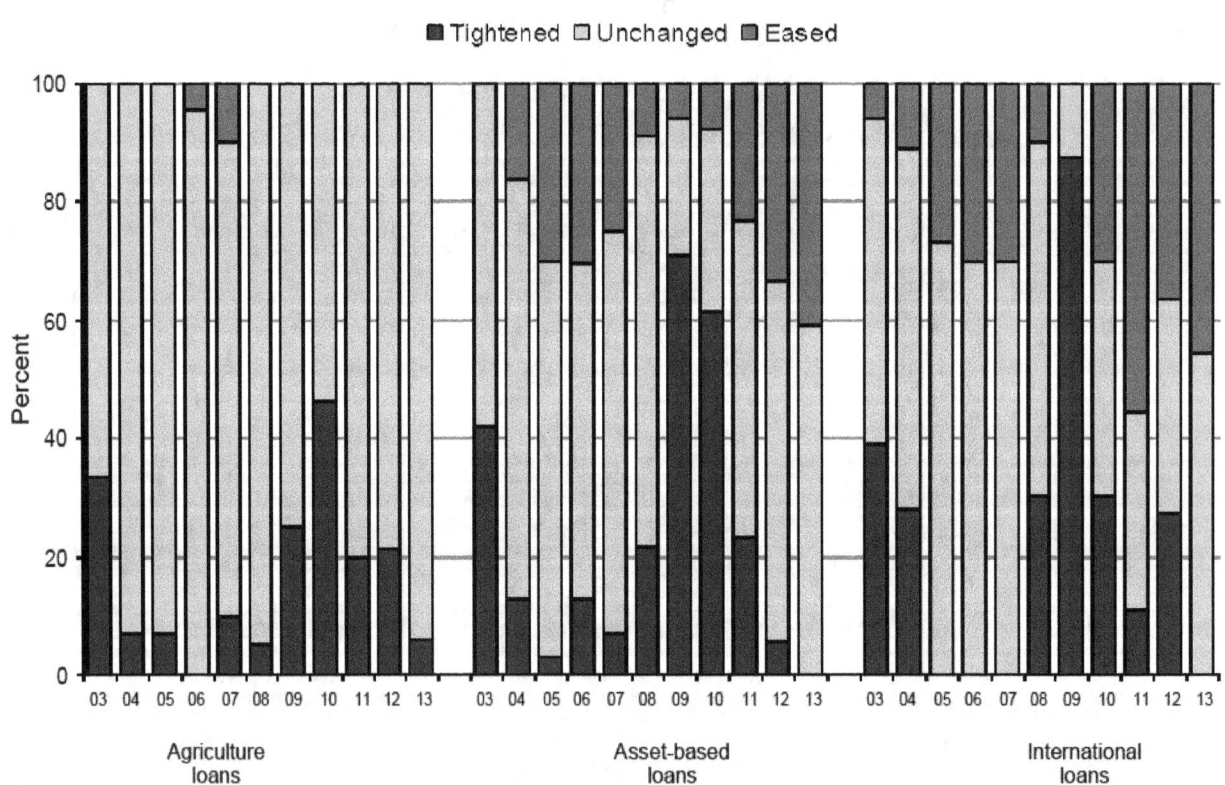

Figure 2 (cont.): Commercial Underwriting Trends, by Product Type

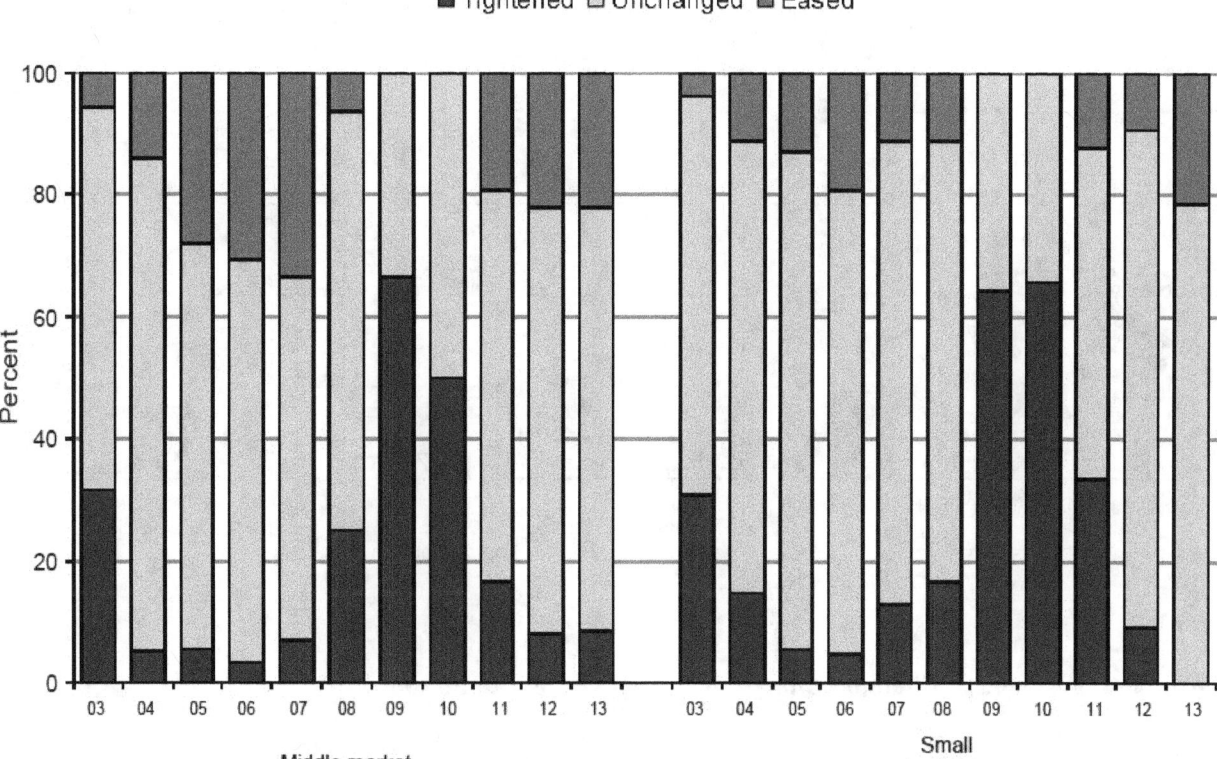

Figure 3: Reasons for Changing Commercial Underwriting Standards

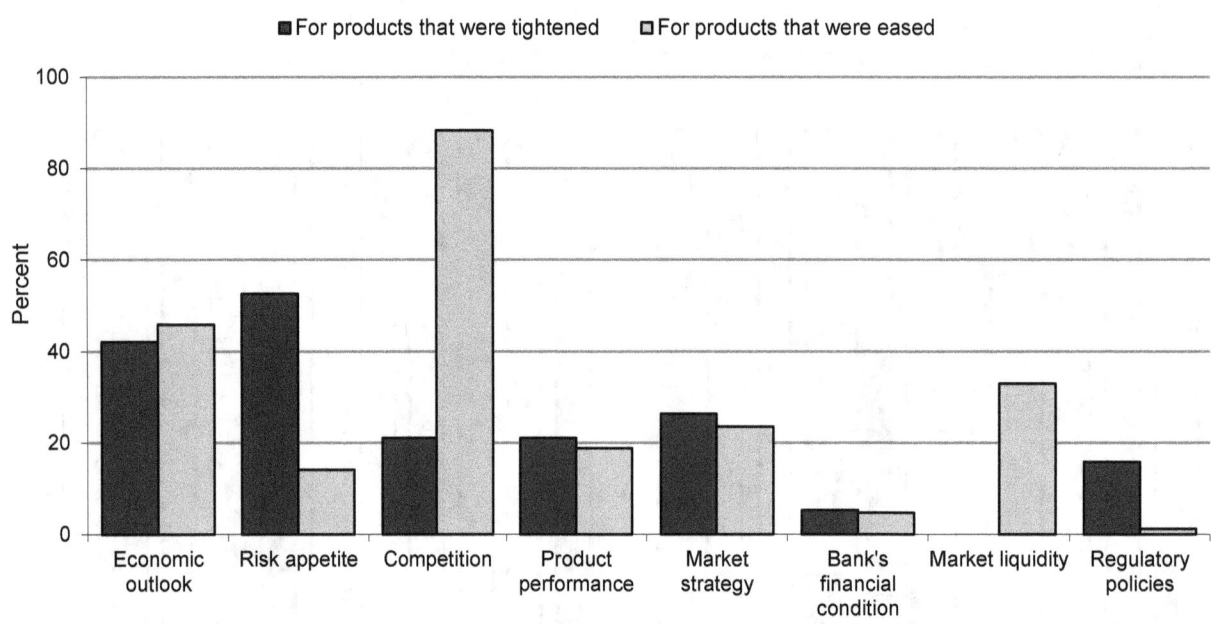

Figure 4: Methods Used to Change Commercial Underwriting Standards

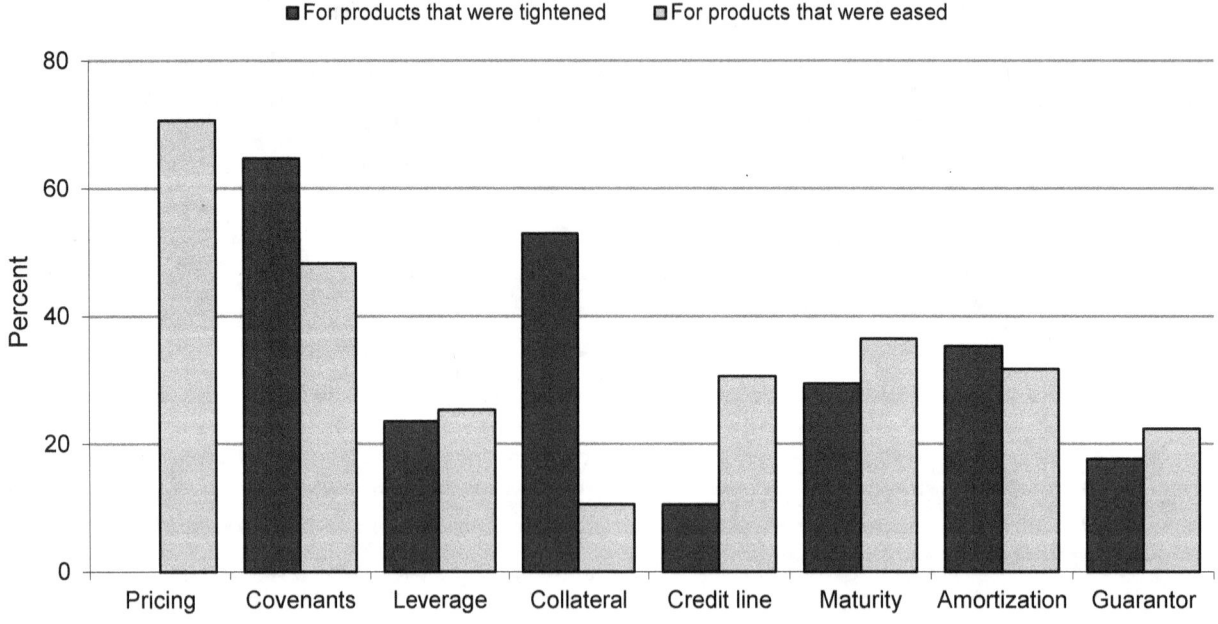

Figure 5: Commercial Credit Risk—Direction of Change and Outlook

Previous 12 months

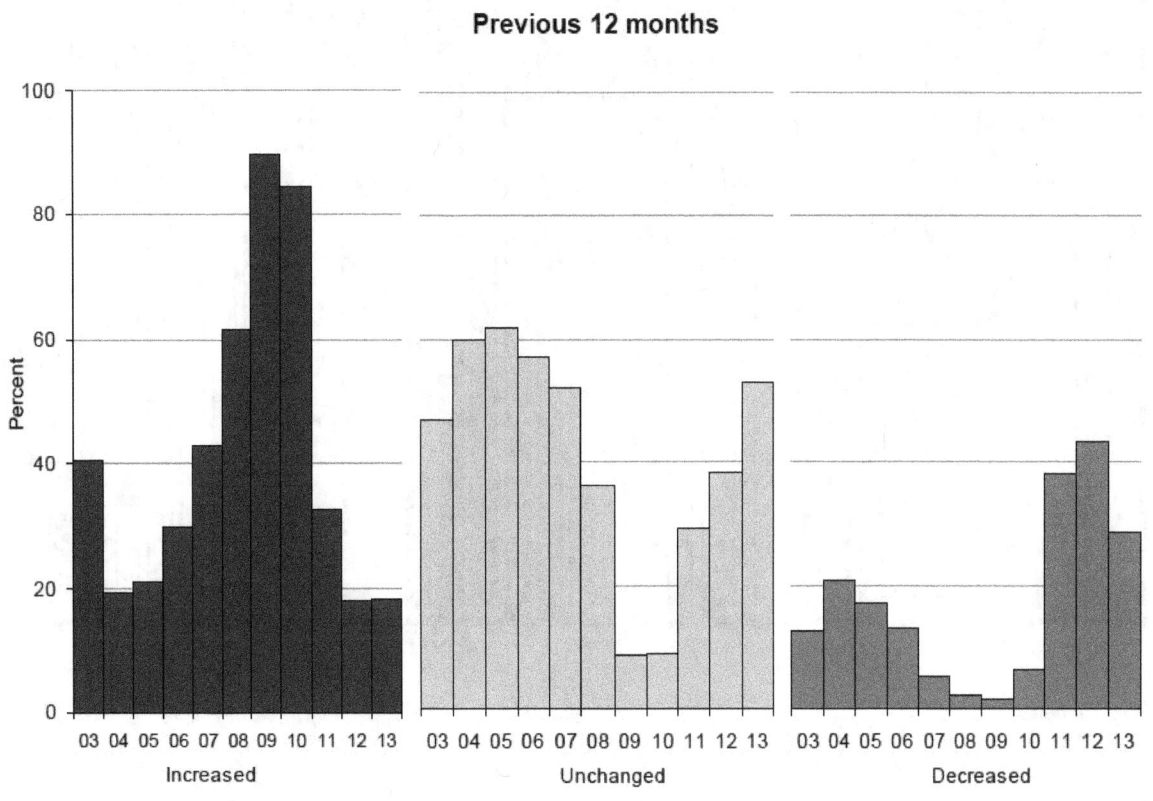

Next 12 months

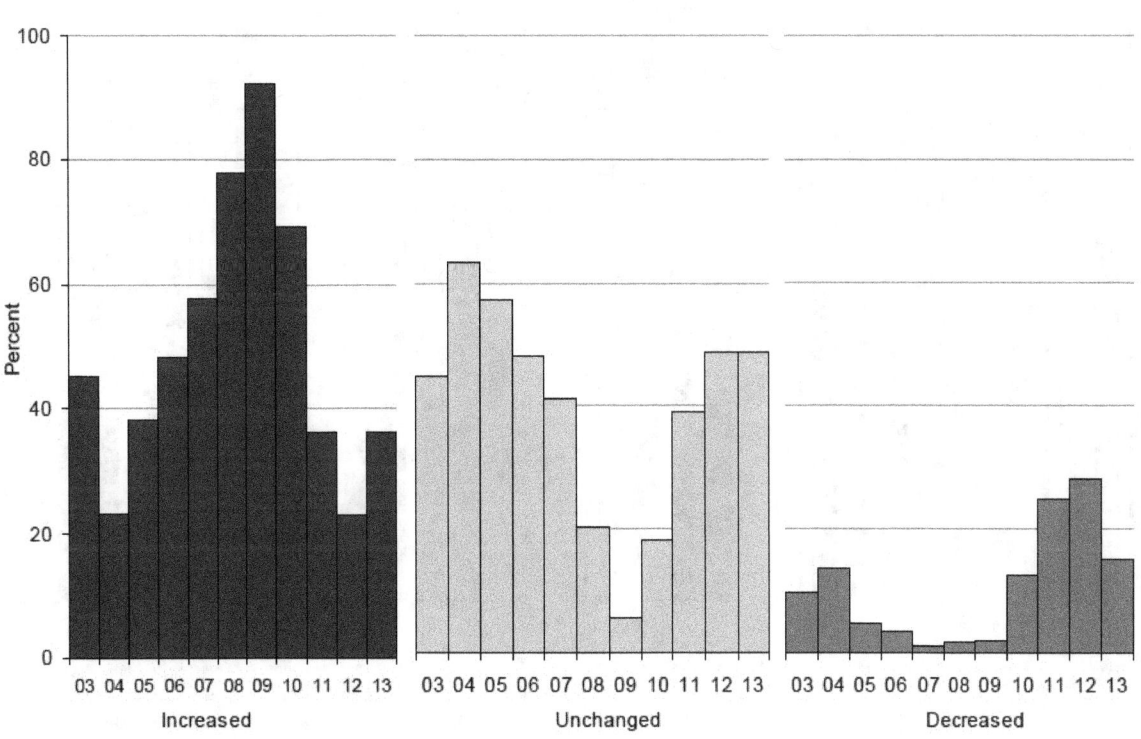

Figure 6: Commercial Credit Risk Trends—Current Credit Risk Change, by Product Type

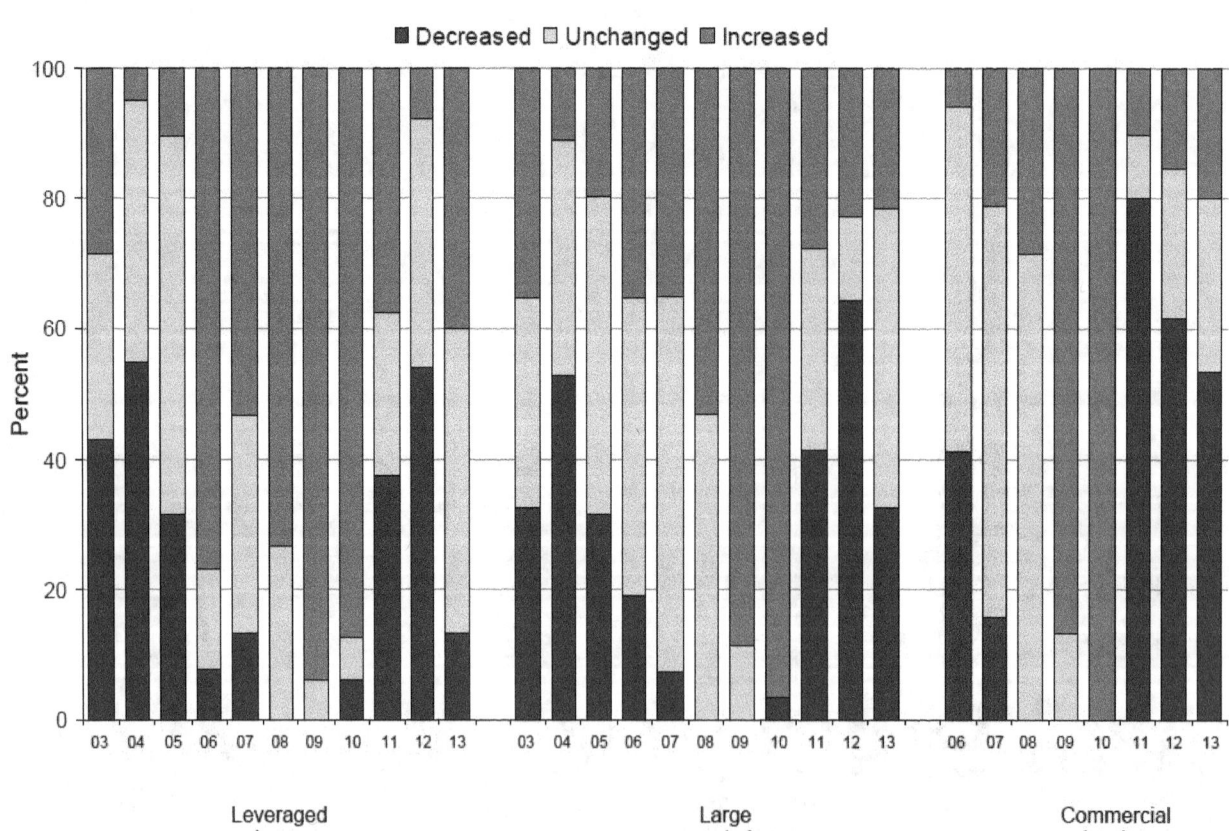

Figure 6 (cont.): Commercial Credit Risk Trends—Current Credit Risk Change, by Product Type

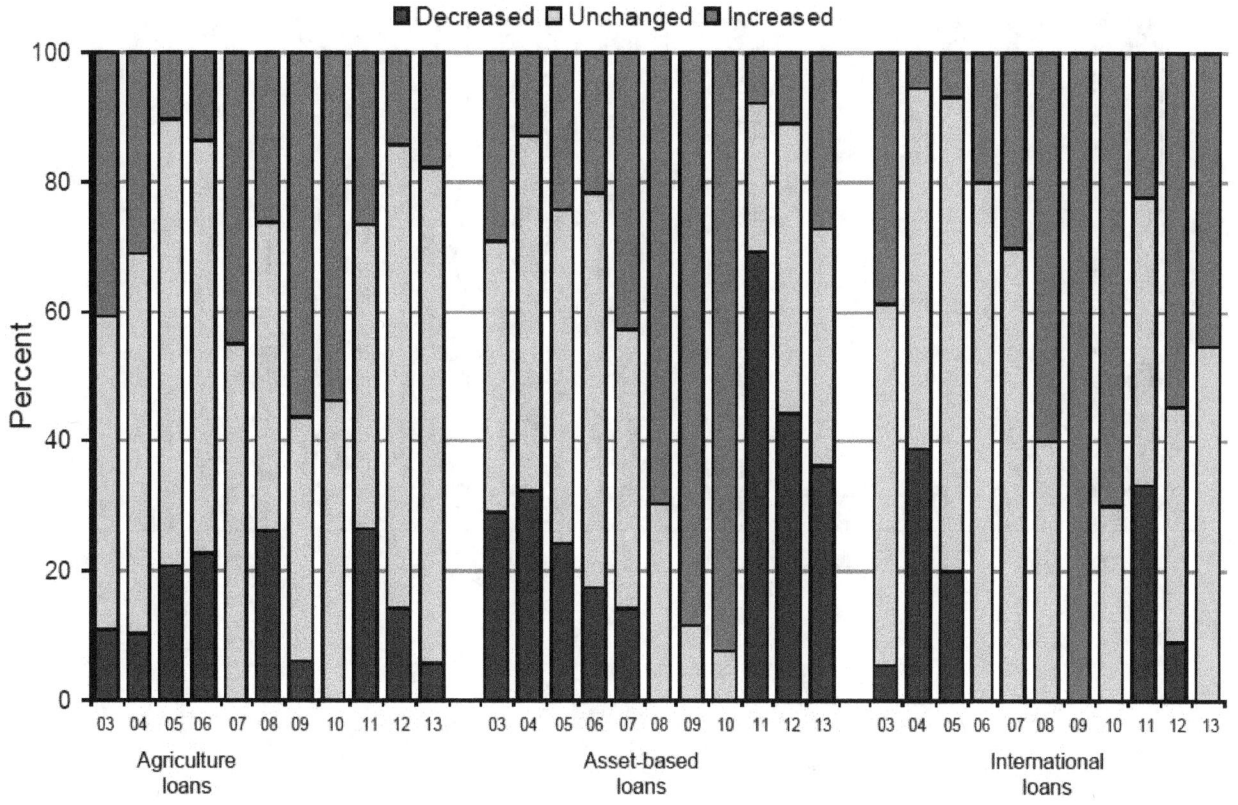

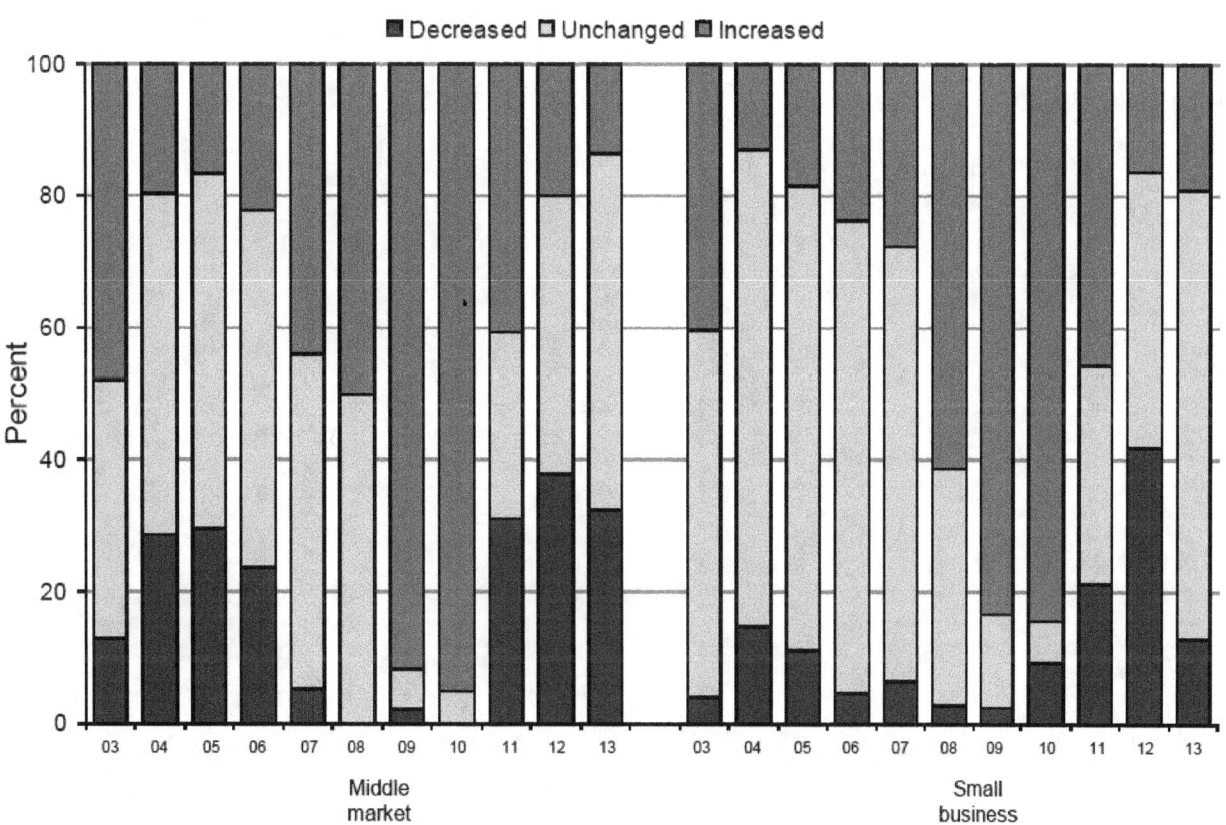

Figure 7: Overall Credit Underwriting Trends—Retail

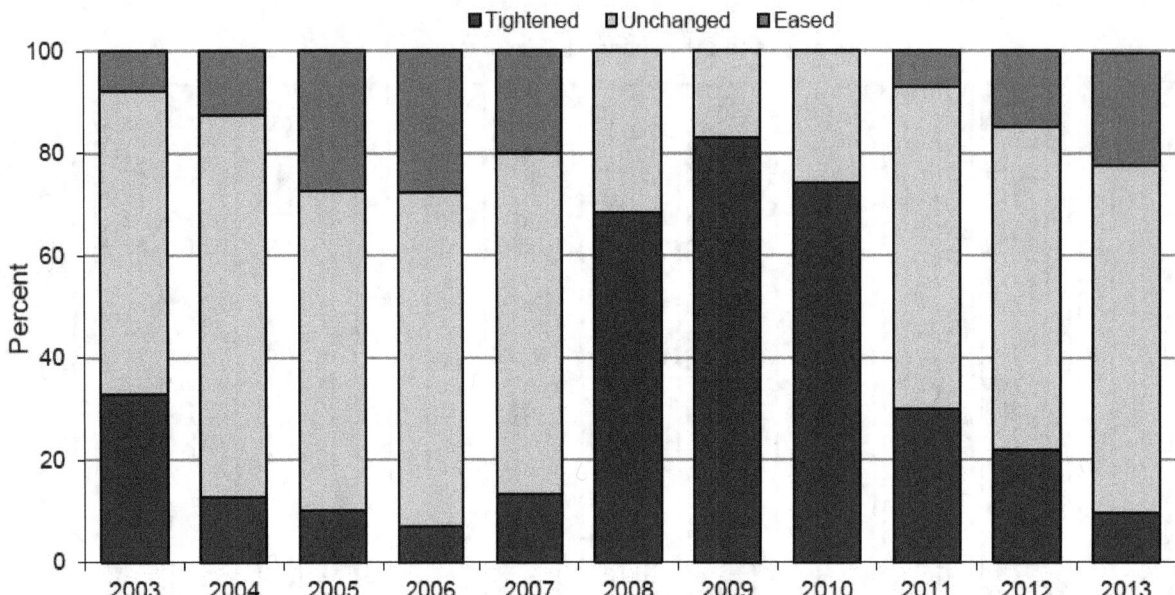

Figure 8: Retail Underwriting Trends, by Product Type

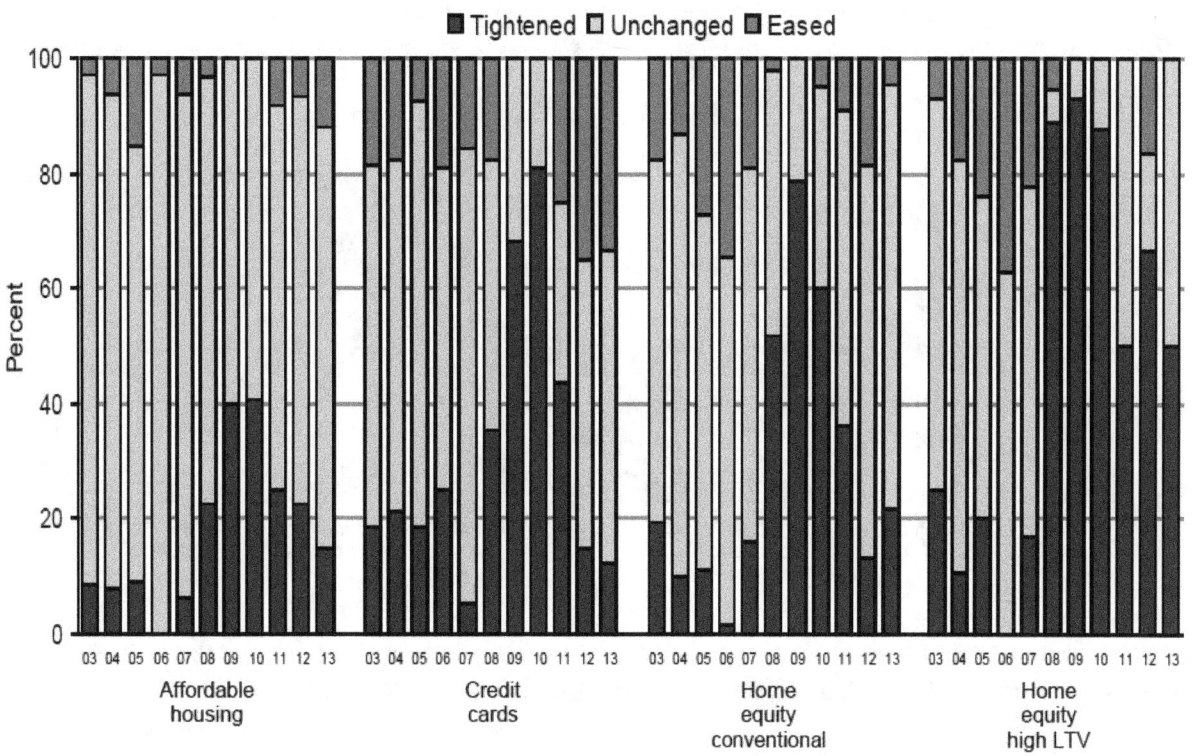

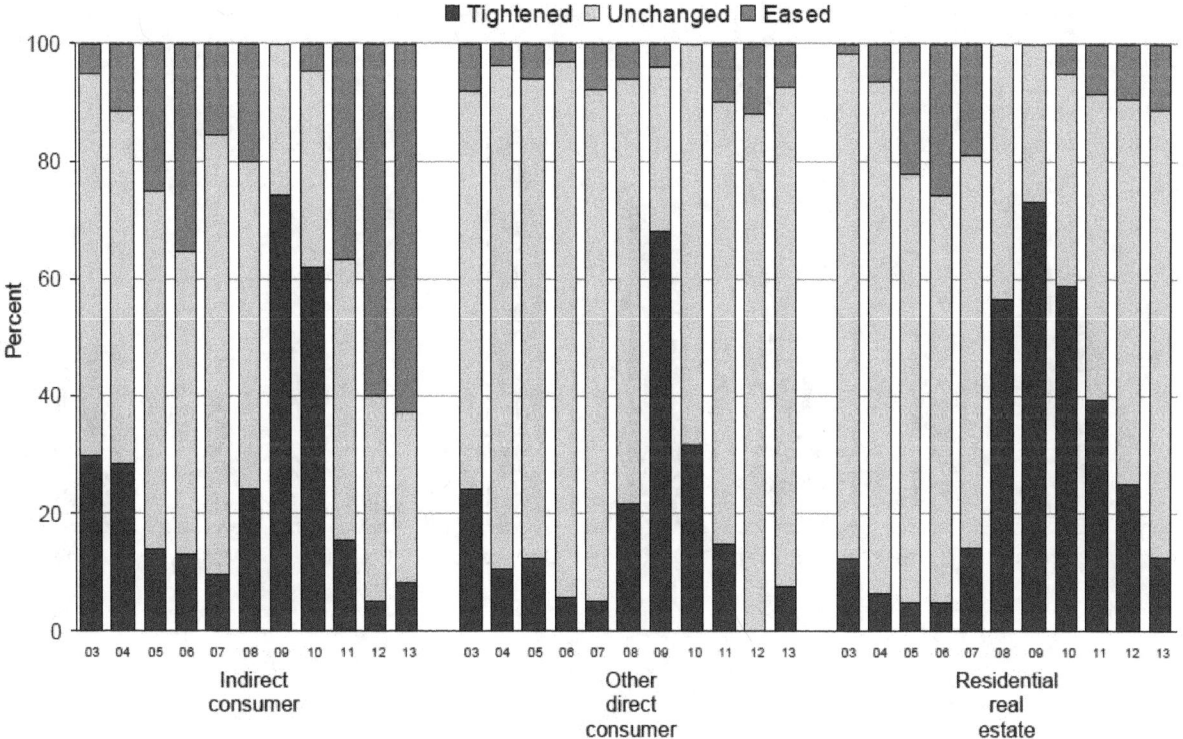

Figure 9: Reasons for Changing Retail Underwriting Standards

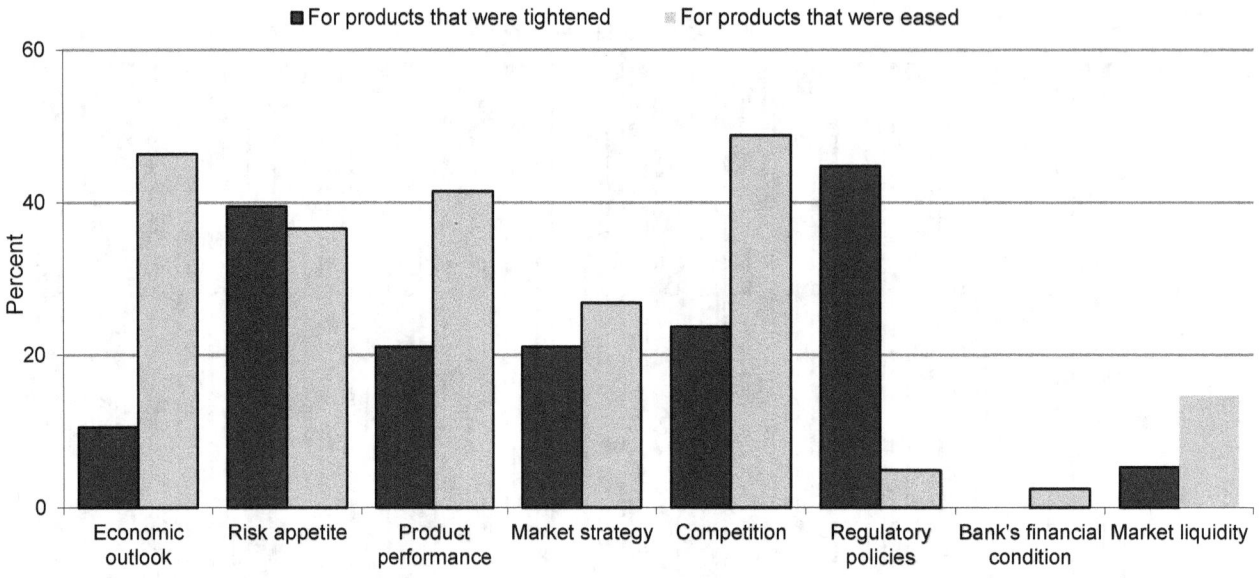

Figure 10: Overall Methods Used to Change Retail Underwriting Standards

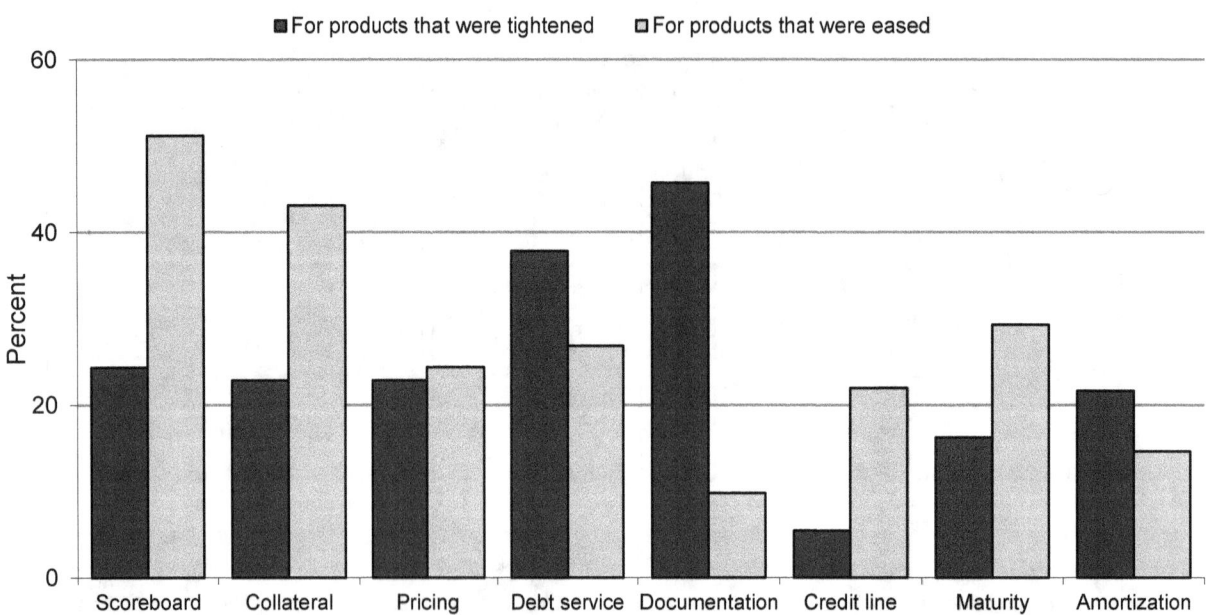

Figure 11: Retail Credit Risk Direction of Change and Outlook

Previous 12 months

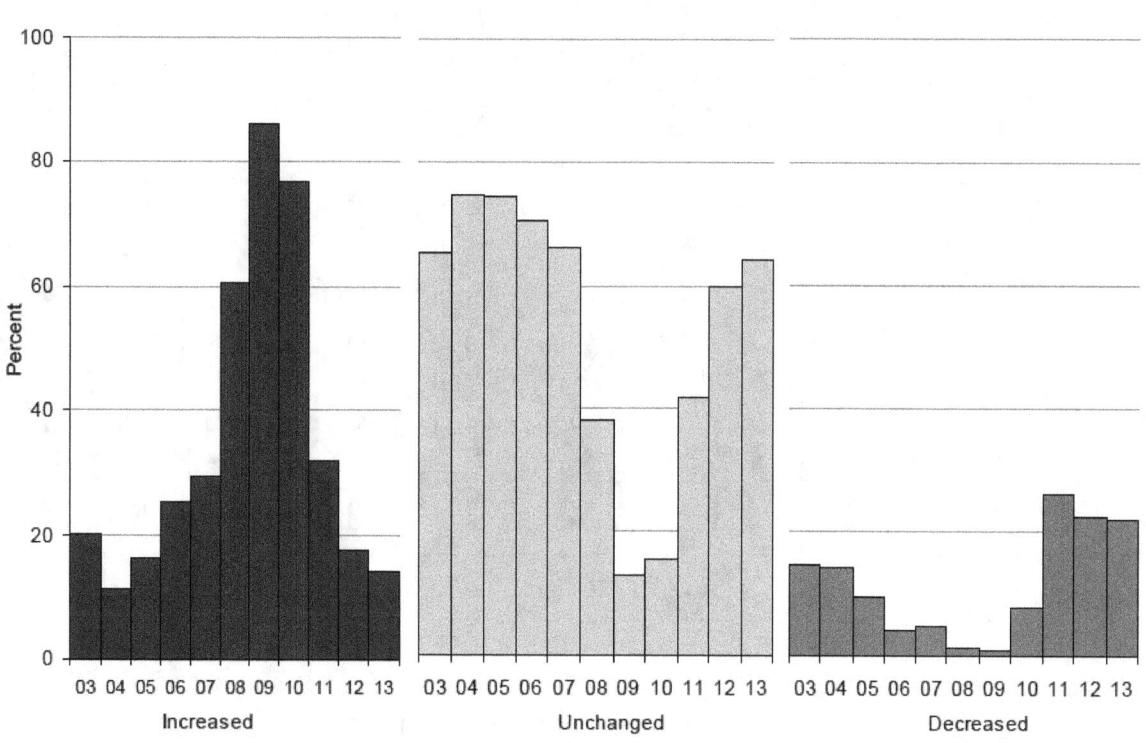

Next 12 months

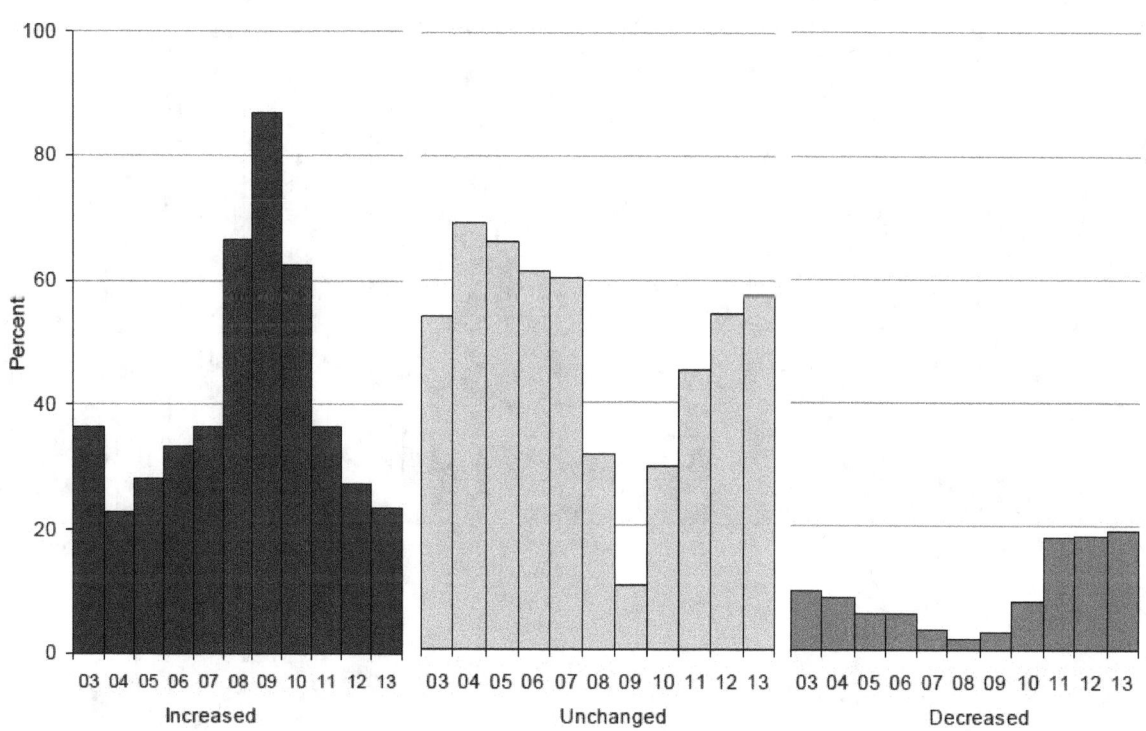

Figure 12: Retail Credit Risk Trends—Current Credit Risk Change, by Product Type

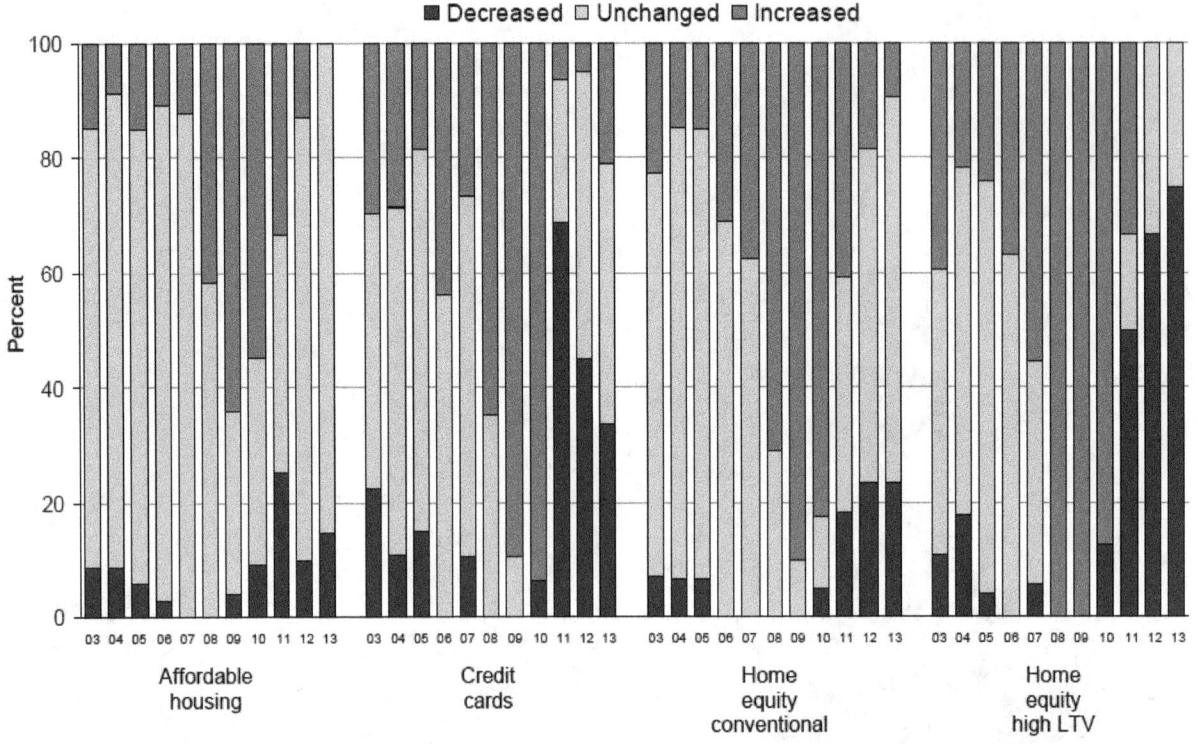

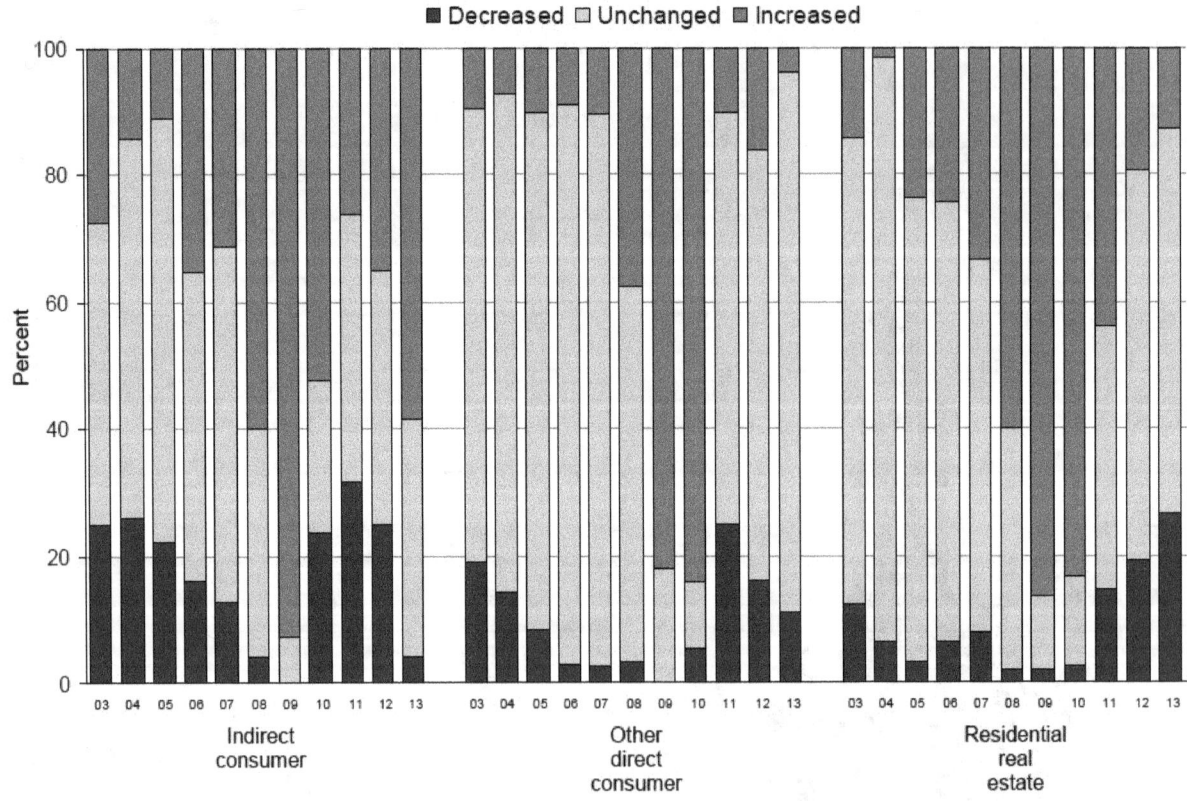

Part III: Data Tables

Some percentages in the following tables do not add to 100 because of rounding.

A. Commercial Lending Portfolios

Agricultural Lending

Sixteen of the 86 surveyed banks met the threshold for reporting on agricultural lending.

Table 15: Changes in Underwriting Standards in Agricultural Loan Portfolios (Percentage of Responses)

Year	Eased	Unchanged	Tightened
2003	0	67	33
2004	0	93	7
2005	0	93	7
2006	5	95	0
2007	10	80	10
2008	0	95	5
2009	0	75	25
2010	0	54	46
2011	0	80	20
2012	0	79	21
2013	0	94	6

Table 16: Changes in the Level of Credit Risk in Agricultural Loan Portfolios (Percentage of Responses)

Year	Declined significantly	Declined somewhat	Unchanged	Increased somewhat	Increased significantly
2003	0	11	48	41	0
2004	0	10	59	31	0
2005	4	17	69	10	0
2006	0	23	63	14	0
2007	0	0	55	45	0
2008	0	26	47	26	0
2009	0	6	38	56	0
2010	0	0	46	31	23
2011	0	27	46	27	0
2012	7	7	72	14	0
2013	0	6	76	18	0
Expected risk in 12 months	0	0	71	29	0

Asset-Based Lending

Twenty-two surveyed banks met the threshold for reporting on asset-based lending.

Table 17: Changes in Underwriting Standards in Asset-Based Loan Portfolios (Percentage of Responses)

Year	Eased	Unchanged	Tightened
2003	0	58	42
2004	16	71	13
2005	30	67	3
2006	30	57	13
2007	25	68	7
2008	8	70	22
2009	6	23	71
2010	8	31	61
2011	23	54	23
2012	33	61	6
2013	41	59	0

Table 18: Changes in the Level of Credit Risk in Asset-Based Loan Portfolios (Percentage of Responses)

Year	Declined significantly	Declined somewhat	Unchanged	Increased somewhat	Increased significantly
2003	3	26	42	29	0
2004	3	29	55	13	0
2005	0	24	52	24	0
2006	0	17	61	22	0
2007	0	14	43	43	0
2008	0	0	30	70	0
2009	0	0	12	70	18
2010	0	0	8	77	15
2011	0	69	23	8	0
2012	11	33	45	11	0
2013	0	36	37	27	0
Expected risk in 12 months	0	5	50	45	0

Commercial Leasing

Sixteen surveyed banks met the threshold for reporting on commercial leasing.

Table 19: Changes in Underwriting Standards in Commercial Leasing Loan Portfolios (Percentage of Responses)

Year	Eased	Unchanged	Tightened
2006	12	76	12
2007	26	69	5
2008	7	50	43
2009	0	40	60
2010	0	27	73
2011	10	60	30
2012	8	77	15
2013	7	93	0

Table 20: Changes in the Level of Credit Risk in Commercial Leasing Loan Portfolios (Percentage of Responses)

Year	Declined significantly	Declined somewhat	Unchanged	Increased somewhat	Increased significantly
2006	6	35	53	6	0
2007	0	16	63	21	0
2008	0	0	71	29	0
2009	0	0	13	80	7
2010	0	0	0	55	45
2011	0	80	10	10	0
2012	0	62	23	15	0
2013	6	47	27	20	0
Expected risk in 12 months	0	0	87	13	0

Commercial Real Estate Lending—Commercial Construction

Thirty-five surveyed banks met the threshold for reporting on commercial construction lending.

Table 21: Changes in Underwriting Standards in Commercial Construction Loan Portfolios (Percentage of Responses)

Year	Eased	Unchanged	Tightened
2003	2	61	37
2004	10	75	15
2005	29	63	8
2006	32	56	12
2007	28	59	13
2008	8	43	49
2009	0	20	80
2010	3	25	72
2011	3	61	36
2012	5	75	20
2013	18	71	11

Table 22: Changes in the Level of Credit Risk in Commercial Construction Loan Portfolios (Percentage of Responses)

Year	Declined significantly	Declined somewhat	Unchanged	Increased somewhat	Increased significantly
2003	0	7	46	42	5
2004	0	7	59	34	0
2005	2	5	65	28	0
2006	0	5	65	30	0
2007	0	2	48	49	1
2008	0	0	22	69	8
2009	0	0	5	54	41
2010	0	5	3	50	42
2011	6	40	18	33	3
2012	8	38	43	8	3
2013	10	24	55	11	0
Expected risk in 12 months	3	32	39	26	0

Commercial Real Estate Lending—Residential Construction

Fourteen surveyed banks met the threshold for reporting on residential construction lending.

Table 23: Changes in Underwriting Standards in Residential Construction Loan Portfolios (Percentage of Responses)

Year	Eased	Unchanged	Tightened
2003	0	76	24
2004	5	86	9
2005	21	72	7
2006	25	64	11
2007	17	50	33
2008	2	36	62
2009	0	8	92
2010	0	36	64
2011	0	63	37
2012	0	79	21
2013	0	92	8

Table 24: Changes in the Level of Credit Risk in Residential Construction Loan Portfolios (Percentage of Responses)

Year	Declined significantly	Declined somewhat	Unchanged	Increased somewhat	Increased significantly
2003	0	2	62	34	2
2004	0	4	76	18	2
2005	2	6	65	27	0
2006	0	2	52	46	0
2007	0	4	27	63	6
2008	0	0	7	48	45
2009	0	0	0	34	66
2010	5	9	4	41	41
2011	5	47	11	32	5
2012	10	32	37	21	0
2013	0	46	54	0	0
Expected risk in 12 months	0	31	31	38	0

Commercial Real Estate Lending—Other

Seventy-five surveyed banks met the threshold for reporting on other commercial real estate lending.

Table 25: Changes in Underwriting Standards in Other Commercial Real Estate Loan Portfolios (Percentage of Responses)

Year	Eased	Unchanged	Tightened
2003	5	71	24
2004	8	83	9
2005	24	65	11
2006	32	60	8
2007	20	73	7
2008	2	73	25
2009	2	22	76
2010	2	38	60
2011	9	58	33
2012	12	76	12
2013	24	68	8

Table 26: Changes in the Level of Credit Risk in Other Commercial Real Estate Loan Portfolios (Percentage of Responses)

Year	Declined significantly	Declined somewhat	Unchanged	Increased somewhat	Increased significantly
2003	0	5	48	43	4
2004	0	12	66	20	2
2005	2	9	65	24	0
2006	1	10	55	34	0
2007	0	2	59	38	1
2008	0	2	38	58	2
2009	0	2	5	67	26
2010	0	2	9	55	34
2011	2	33	33	23	9
2012	8	36	38	15	3
2013	6	27	51	15	1
Expected risk in 12 months	1	25	39	35	0

International Lending

Ten surveyed banks met the threshold for reporting on international lending.

Table 27: Changes in Underwriting Standards in International Loan Portfolios (Percentage of Responses)

Year	Eased	Unchanged	Tightened
2003	6	55	39
2004	11	61	28
2005	27	73	0
2006	30	70	0
2007	30	70	0
2008	10	60	30
2009	0	13	87
2010	30	40	30
2011	56	33	11
2012	36	36	27
2013	45	55	0

Table 28: Changes in the Level of Credit Risk in International Loan Portfolios (Percentage of Responses)

Year	Declined significantly	Declined somewhat	Unchanged	Increased somewhat	Increased significantly
2003	0	6	55	33	6
2004	6	33	55	6	0
2005	0	20	73	7	0
2006	0	0	80	20	0
2007	0	0	70	30	0
2008	0	0	40	40	20
2009	0	0	0	63	37
2010	0	0	30	50	20
2011	0	33	45	22	0
2012	0	9	36	55	0
2013	0	0	55	45	0
Expected risk in 12 months	0	0	45	55	0

Large Corporate Lending

Thirty-seven surveyed banks met the threshold for reporting on large corporate loans.

Table 29: Changes in Underwriting Standards in Large Corporate Loan Portfolios (Percentage of Responses)

Year	Eased	Unchanged	Tightened
2003	3	49	48
2004	17	66	17
2005	32	68	0
2006	49	51	0
2007	40	60	0
2008	6	62	32
2009	0	40	60
2010	3	38	59
2011	38	55	7
2012	32	58	10
2013	38	57	5

Table 30: Changes in the Level of Credit Risk in Large Corporate Loan Portfolios (Percentage of Responses)

Year	Declined significantly	Declined somewhat	Unchanged	Increased somewhat	Increased significantly
2003	5	27	33	30	5
2004	17	36	36	11	0
2005	5	27	49	19	0
2006	0	19	46	32	3
2007	0	8	57	35	0
2008	0	0	47	47	6
2009	0	0	12	77	11
2010	0	3	0	76	21
2011	0	41	31	28	0
2012	10	55	13	19	3
2013	0	32	46	22	0
Expected risk in 12 months	0	5	49	46	0

Leveraged Lending

Sixteen surveyed banks met the threshold for reporting on leveraged loans.

Table 31: Changes in Underwriting Standards in Leveraged Loan Portfolios (Percentage of Responses)

Year	Eased	Unchanged	Tightened
2003	0	48	52
2004	15	85	0
2005	32	68	0
2006	61	31	8
2007	67	33	0
2008	20	20	60
2009	0	31	69
2010	0	25	75
2011	37	44	19
2012	38	62	0
2013	53	47	0

Table 32: Changes in the Level of Credit Risk in Leveraged Loan Portfolios (Percentage of Responses)

Year	Declined significantly	Declined somewhat	Unchanged	Increased somewhat	Increased significantly
2003	10	33	28	29	0
2004	15	40	40	5	0
2005	5	27	58	5	5
2006	0	8	15	69	8
2007	0	13	34	53	0
2008	0	0	27	53	20
2009	0	0	6	63	31
2010	0	6	6	63	25
2011	0	38	25	31	6
2012	8	46	38	0	0
2013	0	13	47	40	0
Expected risk in 12 months	0	7	26	67	0

Middle Market Lending

Fifty-eight surveyed banks met the threshold for reporting on middle market lending.

Table 33: Changes in Underwriting Standards in Middle Market Loan Portfolios (Percentage of Responses)

Year	Eased	Unchanged	Tightened
2003	6	63	31
2004	14	81	5
2005	28	67	5
2006	31	66	3
2007	33	60	7
2008	6	69	25
2009	0	33	67
2010	0	50	50
2011	19	64	17
2012	22	70	8
2013	22	70	8

Table 34: Changes in the Level of Credit Risk in Middle Market Loan Portfolios (Percentage of Responses)

Year	Declined significantly	Declined somewhat	Unchanged	Increased somewhat	Increased significantly
2003	0	13	39	44	4
2004	0	28	52	18	2
2005	4	26	54	16	0
2006	0	24	54	20	2
2007	0	5	51	44	0
2008	0	0	50	48	2
2009	0	2	6	88	4
2010	0	0	5	73	22
2011	0	31	29	38	2
2012	4	34	42	16	4
2013	0	32	54	12	2
Expected risk in 12 months	0	10	56	34	0

Small Business Lending

Forty-five surveyed banks met the threshold for reporting on small business lending.

Table 35: Changes in Underwriting Standards in Small Business Loan Portfolios (Percentage of Responses)

Year	Eased	Unchanged	Tightened
2003	4	65	31
2004	11	74	15
2005	13	81	6
2006	19	76	5
2007	11	76	13
2008	11	72	17
2009	0	36	64
2010	0	34	66
2011	12	55	33
2012	9	82	9
2013	21	79	0

Table 36: Changes in the Level of Credit Risk in Small Business Loan Portfolios (Percentage of Responses)

Year	Declined significantly	Declined somewhat	Unchanged	Increased somewhat	Increased significantly
2003	0	4	56	38	2
2004	0	15	72	13	0
2005	0	11	70	19	0
2006	0	5	71	22	2
2007	2	4	66	26	2
2008	0	3	36	58	3
2009	0	2	14	72	12
2010	0	9	6	66	19
2011	0	21	33	46	0
2012	2	40	42	16	0
2013	0	13	68	19	0
Expected risk in 12 months	0	13	55	30	2

B. Retail Lending Portfolios

Affordable Housing Lending

Thirty-two surveyed banks met the threshold for reporting on affordable housing lending.

Table 37: Changes in Underwriting Standards in Affordable Housing Loan Portfolios (Percentage of Responses)

Year	Eased	Unchanged	Tightened
2003	3	88	9
2004	6	86	8
2005	15	76	9
2006	3	97	0
2007	6	88	6
2008	3	74	23
2009	0	60	40
2010	0	59	41
2011	8	67	25
2012	6	71	23
2013	12	73	15

Table 38: Changes in the Level of Credit Risk in Affordable Housing Loan Portfolios (Percentage of Responses)

Year	Declined significantly	Declined somewhat	Unchanged	Increased somewhat	Increased significantly
2003	0	9	76	15	0
2004	0	9	82	9	0
2005	0	6	79	15	0
2006	0	3	86	11	0
2007	0	0	88	12	0
2008	0	0	58	35	6
2009	0	4	32	52	12
2010	0	9	36	46	9
2011	0	25	42	33	0
2012	0	10	77	13	0
2013	3	12	85	0	0
Expected risk in 12 months	0	12	79	9	0

Conventional Home Equity Lending

Sixty-three surveyed banks met the threshold for reporting on conventional home equity lending.

Table 39: Changes in Underwriting Standards in Conventional Home Equity Loan Portfolios (Percentage of Responses)

Year	Eased	Unchanged	Tightened
2003	18	63	19
2004	13	77	10
2005	27	62	11
2006	34	64	2
2007	19	65	16
2008	2	46	52
2009	0	22	78
2010	5	35	60
2011	9	55	36
2012	18	68	14
2013	5	73	22

Table 40: Changes in the Level of Credit Risk in Conventional Home Equity Loan Portfolios (Percentage of Responses)

Year	Declined significantly	Declined somewhat	Unchanged	Increased somewhat	Increased significantly
2003	4	4	69	23	0
2004	0	6	79	13	2
2005	0	7	78	15	0
2006	0	0	69	29	2
2007	0	0	63	34	3
2008	0	0	29	52	19
2009	0	0	10	63	27
2010	0	5	12	73	10
2011	0	18	41	41	0
2012	0	23	58	18	0
2013	0	24	67	9	0
Expected risk in 12 months	2	23	62	11	2

Credit Card Lending

Twenty-one surveyed banks met the threshold for reporting on credit card lending.

Table 41: Changes in Underwriting Standards in Credit Card Loan Portfolios (Percentage of Responses)

Year	Eased	Unchanged	Tightened
2003	19	62	19
2004	18	61	21
2005	7	74	19
2006	19	56	25
2007	16	79	5
2008	18	47	35
2009	0	32	68
2010	0	19	81
2011	25	31	44
2012	35	50	15
2013	33	54	13

Table 42: Changes in the Level of Credit Risk in Credit Card Loan Portfolios (Percentage of Responses)

Year	Declined significantly	Declined somewhat	Unchanged	Increased somewhat	Increased significantly
2003	0	22	48	30	0
2004	0	11	61	25	3
2005	0	15	67	18	0
2006	0	0	56	44	0
2007	0	11	63	26	0
2008	0	0	35	65	0
2009	0	0	10	53	37
2010	0	6	0	63	31
2011	0	69	25	0	6
2012	15	30	50	5	0
2013	0	33	46	17	4
Expected risk in 12 months	0	13	50	37	0

Direct Consumer Lending

Twenty-five surveyed banks met the threshold for reporting on other direct consumer lending.

Table 43: Changes in Underwriting Standards in Other Direct Consumer Loan Portfolios (Percentage of Responses)

Year	Eased	Unchanged	Tightened
2003	8	68	24
2004	3	86	11
2005	6	82	12
2006	3	91	6
2007	8	87	5
2008	6	72	22
2009	4	28	68
2010	0	68	32
2011	10	75	15
2012	12	88	0
2013	8	85	7

Table 44: Changes in the Level of Credit Risk in Other Direct Consumer Loan Portfolios (Percentage of Responses)

Year	Declined significantly	Declined somewhat	Unchanged	Increased somewhat	Increased significantly
2003	2	17	72	7	2
2004	2	13	78	7	0
2005	0	8	82	10	0
2006	0	3	88	9	0
2007	0	3	87	10	0
2008	0	3	59	38	0
2009	0	0	18	68	14
2010	0	5	11	74	10
2011	0	25	65	10	0
2012	4	12	68	16	0
2013	0	11	85	4	0
Expected risk in 12 months	0	4	78	18	0

High Loan-to-Value Home Equity Lending

Two surveyed banks met the threshold for reporting on HLTV home equity lending.

Table 45: Changes in Underwriting Standards in HLTV Home Equity Loan Portfolios (Percentage of Responses)

Year	Eased	Unchanged	Tightened
2003	7	68	25
2004	18	71	11
2005	24	56	20
2006	37	63	0
2007	22	61	17
2008	6	6	89
2009	0	7	93
2010	0	13	87
2011	0	50	50
2012	17	17	66
2013	0	50	50

Table 46: Changes in the Level of Credit Risk in HLTV Home Equity Loan Portfolios (Percentage of Responses)

Year	Declined significantly	Declined somewhat	Unchanged	Increased somewhat	Increased significantly
2003	0	11	50	36	3
2004	0	18	61	18	3
2005	0	4	72	24	0
2006	0	0	63	37	0
2007	0	6	39	55	0
2008	0	0	0	56	44
2009	0	0	0	36	64
2010	0	13	0	50	37
2011	17	33	17	33	0
2012	0	67	33	0	0
2013	0	75	25	0	0
Expected risk in 12 months	0	50	50	0	0

Indirect Consumer Lending

Twenty-four surveyed banks met the threshold for reporting on indirect consumer lending.

Table 47: Changes in Underwriting Standards in Indirect Consumer Loan Portfolios (Percentage of Responses)

Year	Eased	Unchanged	Tightened
2003	5	65	30
2004	11	60	29
2005	25	61	14
2006	35	52	13
2007	16	75	9
2008	20	56	24
2009	0	26	74
2010	5	33	62
2011	37	47	16
2012	60	35	5
2013	63	29	8

Table 48: Changes in the Level of Credit Risk in Indirect Consumer Loan Portfolios (Percentage of Responses)

Year	Declined significantly	Declined somewhat	Unchanged	Increased somewhat	Increased significantly
2003	5	20	47	28	0
2004	0	26	60	14	0
2005	3	19	67	8	3
2006	6	10	48	36	0
2007	0	3	87	10	0
2008	0	4	36	60	0
2009	0	0	7	74	19
2010	0	24	24	47	5
2011	0	32	42	26	0
2012	0	25	40	35	0
2013	0	4	38	58	0
Expected risk in 12 months	0	9	25	58	8

Residential Real Estate Lending

Seventy-eight surveyed banks met the threshold for reporting on residential real estate lending.

Table 49: Changes in Underwriting Standards in Residential Real Estate Loan Portfolios (Percentage of Responses)

Year	Eased	Unchanged	Tightened
2003	2	86	12
2004	7	86	7
2005	22	73	5
2006	26	69	5
2007	19	67	14
2008	0	44	56
2009	0	27	73
2010	5	36	59
2011	8	52	40
2012	10	65	25
2013	11	76	13

Table 50: Changes in the Level of Credit Risk in Residential Real Estate Loan Portfolios (Percentage of Responses)

Year	Declined significantly	Declined somewhat	Unchanged	Increased somewhat	Increased significantly
2003	0	12	74	12	2
2004	0	6	92	2	0
2005	0	3	73	24	0
2006	0	7	69	24	0
2007	2	6	59	33	0
2008	2	0	38	55	5
2009	0	2	12	69	17
2010	0	3	14	57	26
2011	0	15	42	39	4
2012	1	18	62	19	0
2013	1	25	61	13	0
Expected risk in 12 months	3	24	49	24	0